GRIEF WORK

PRESENTED TO:
MRS. MAISIE WREN

BY:

GRIEF WORK

VELMA D. STEVENS

BROADMAN PRESS
NASHVILLE, TENNESSEE

ISBN: 0-8054-5088-2
Dewey Decimal Classification: 301.42
Subject Heading: JOY AND SORROW // WIDOWED PEOPLE // DEATH
Library of Congress Card Catalog Number: 89-38487
Printed in the United States of America

Library of Congress Cataloging-in-Publication Data

Stevens, Velma Darbo.
   [After weeping, a song. Chapters 1-4]
   Grief work / Velma D. Brown.
     p. cm.
   Reprint of the first 4 chapters of *After Weeping, a Song* published
in 1980.
   ISBN: 0-8054-5088-2 :
   1. Bereavement--Religious aspects--Christianity. 2. Grief-
-Religious aspects--Christianity. 3. Consolation. I. Title.
BV4905.2.S728 1990
248.8'6--dc20

                                         89-38487
                                            CIP

Contents

Introduction:
The Pilgrimage of Grief

Writing a book about grief is a good deal like giving directions to someone who is going to travel by car in a foreign country. For grief is not a happening. It is a pilgrimage.

A person intending to travel by car in rural England, for instance, can get advice in several ways. He may talk with someone who has made such a trip. From that person he will get a detailed description of the route that was taken, the sights seen, and the problems encountered. But he will know only about that one person's travels.

Or the prospective traveler may go to a travel agent. The travel agent may never have been in the country himself. But he can provide a road map and general instructions about how to travel by car in England.

The best help for the prospective traveler is probably an experienced travel guide. This would be a person with general information about driving in England. He could provide the road map and the instructions. But also, he would have made at least one trip through England and could describe what touring England by car is like. The new traveler would not follow the same route exactly, but such a description would tell the traveler what to expect on a similar journey.

In this book I have tried to act as an "experienced travel guide." I have been widowed twice: once in 1973 and again in 1986. I wrote my first book *After Weeping, a Song* some years after the death of my first husband. I did extensive research into the psychology of grief in the process of writing that book. Although my experiences did not exactly parallel my studies, I found that what I learned and what I lived had much in common.

After the death of my second husband, I experienced grief in somewhat different ways than I had earlier. But again, the stages and process of "grief work" were in line with what we know about bereavement and the restoration to life of the bereft person.

So I have tried to provide a "road map" of the territory of grief. From my study, my experiences, and my observation of other widowed persons, I have outlined the emotions of grief and the stages of grief. I hope that this "road map" will help all who suffer the loss of a mate.

This suffering is probably the most emotionally painful that any human being has to endure. But most of us are acquainted with grief in some measure before that time comes. Grief has been defined as the response of emotional pain to the loss of a significant other. Each time that we have lost someone or something of value to us, we have suffered emotional pain. These griefs, as they are endured, teach us lessons that we can apply to the next significant loss.

One night I was speaking in a church service regarding the emotions of grief. At the end of the question-and-answer period, a pretty, red-haired, nine-year-old girl said to the pastor, "Please, can I ask the lady a question?"

"Of course you can," he replied.

She fixed her blue eyes intently on me and said: "Those things you said you feel when you lose somebody, is it the same when you lose your cat?"

"Yes," I answered. "It's just the same."

She was beginning to learn about grief at

a young age. I hope that, as she grows, she can apply that learning when she loses boyfriends, moves away from familiar friends, and when, in time, she may lose a husband by death.

A trip through a rural countryside is like a pilgrimage of grief in another way. It is not like driving the interstate highways, where one gets on the highway at a certain point and drives straight through to another point. It is more like meandering through small towns, driving along roads which have unexpected potholes and detours. There will be several possible routes between intermediate towns. But the final destination will be the same.

The pilgrimage of grief also has a definite beginning. That is the death of the mate or the time in a terminal illness when death is seen as inevitable. There are varying ways to take the pilgrimage. No two persons take it alike. But the end is the same—it is the entrance into new life.

I do not believe that we talk enough about this final destination. All too many widows whom I have known seem to stop short of the "promised land" of new life for themselves. They may become resigned to the deaths of their wives/husbands. But they never move beyond that stage to the new life.

Myron Madden calls grief "a process through which we are able to separate or draw a line between death and life, [and] it helps us remove death from our lives."[1]

Removing death from our lives is a part of God's plan for his children. If we do not, we may make an idol of the dead person. God's purpose is that we shall live life to the full, whatever happens. Those who give themselves to the painful process of grief, trusting God for guidance and healing, come out at the end of the journey to a new appreciation for life and a new zest for living.

So there are two purposes for grief. One is to mark the passing of a person who has been deeply significant to us. Some time ago I found the reprint of an article by Virginia Barckley, RN, entitled "Grief, a Part of Living." In it she says:

> All grief must not be thought of as dreary and destructive. The world would be worse without it. If no man's life were significant enough to cause weeping, if birth and death were unmarked, if the measure of our years on earth were nothing, we might better be house flies rather

than human beings, made in God's image. Profound grief is preceded by deep love which gives life meaning. In the deepest sense, our days would be empty and futile if we never grieved, or never, dying, left emotional chaos behind us.[2]

The second purpose for grief is equally important. It is to bring us out of "emotional chaos" to new fullness of life. Only those who have made the full pilgrimage of grief, I believe, can truly appreciate and appropriate the gift of life itself.

1
The Emotions of Grief

Grief is individual, but it is also universal. When I lead conferences for bereaved persons and discuss the reactions involved in grief, a typical response is: "Oh, yes, I experienced that. But I didn't know other people did."

Simply knowing that these reactions are part of the human response to a great loss is reassuring to many mourners. One woman, who had been suffering depression, said to me after a conference on grief work: "I'm so relieved to hear that depression is normal. I was beginning to think I was losing my faith, or maybe my mind."

The reactions experienced in grief are generally these:

Shock, disbelief, and numbness
Sorrow
Loss of meaning
Anger, hostility, and guilt
Fear

Loneliness

Depression

Acceptance, resignation, and peace.

The shock reaction belongs to the beginning of the grief process, while complete acceptance signifies the end of the process. But all the other reactions will be felt at different times. They may also appear in various "mixes" during the grief process. In fact, one of the most disturbing characteristics of grief reactions is their tendency to resurface just as the person considers that he/she has gotten past that stage. Anger may disappear and reappear. Waves of weeping may diminish, only to sweep back over the person when they are least expected.

The person may even believe that he/she has reached the place of acceptance and peace, only to have new episodes of loneliness, sorrow, or depression. Not until acceptance has been experienced for a certain period of time, without the intrusion of the other grief reactions, can the mourner be sure that the grief work is really done.

Shock and numbness are the initial reactions to the death of a loved one. The personality reacts to this extreme loss much the same way that the body reacts to a traumatic accident. When, for instance, a part of the body is severed or much blood is lost, the person goes into shock. This is the body's way of protecting itself in a severe trauma. The personality has a similar built-in system of protection. One's mind and emotions are not able to take in the stunning blow of the death of a loved one. And the more sudden and unexpected the death, the greater will be the shock reaction.

Under such circumstances it is fairly common to see bereaved persons acting calmly and even cheerfully in the first few days after the death, even through the funeral. But the observers should not be deceived. The seeming stoicism and acceptance are very likely the result of shock and bewilderment. The person has not yet taken in the extent of the loss and is therefore not yet reacting to it.

Shock may be coupled with bewilderment, disbelief, and even denial of what has happened. This reaction will last until the widowed person begins to realize fully what has taken place.

The shock reaction comes either at the time of death or at the time when a person knows that the partner is going to die, as in a terminal illness. In both cases the reaction will be the same. But the one who knows of an impending death will have more time to prepare for it.

Sorrow is the reaction of painful longing for the lost mate. It is characterized by sharp emotional pain, weeping, sobbing, and even moaning. This reaction is so familiar that many people think of it as the total grief reaction.

Sorrow comes as the widowed person begins to take in the extent of the loss. A very close relationship enhances the personalities of both partners. It brings security, joy, companionship, and a share in decision-making and in the life-sustaining processes of life. When such a relationship is broken, as by the death of one partner, the sense of loss is acute. It seems as if a part of the living person has been cut off.

Imagine a person who has lost a leg, trying painfully to get around with just one. Every move by such an amputee reminds him of his lost member. So every attempt of the bereaved person to go on with life brings acute reminders of the lost partner. Women say that setting a table with one less place is terribly painful. Men say that coming home to an empty house is agony.

Sorrow is most acute during the first weeks after the death. Later the waves of sorrow may not come so often, but they still occur when something reminds the widow of the lost loved one. The reminder may be unexpected, such as hearing a wife's favorite music or seeing a stranger who somehow resembles the dead husband. At such times it is particularly hard to deal with the sorrow because the bereaved person's defenses are down.

Loss of meaning refers to loss of status and self-worth that comes with the death of a mate. It is painful to be be labeled "widow" or "widower" after proudly bearing the title "wife" or "husband." Even with all the advances in equal rights between the sexes and affirmations of individual worth, in modern America marriage still confers status. Persons still ask about a family relation, "When is he/she going to get married?" And if a persons delays marriage into the thirties, eyebrows begin to be raised. "What's wrong with this person that he/she doesn't get married?" is the implicit question.

So to be catapulted out of a desirable social status into a marital wasteland can be devastating. Persons know how to be husbands or wives. No one knows how to be a widow or widower.

Loss of meaning goes beyond status, however. Much of our self-worth comes from what we do every day. Most of the usual tasks we perform are in relation to our spouses. Many women cook, clean, shop, and wash for the benefit of their husbands.Many men care for the lawn, keep the cars in running order, and do repairs around the house for the benefit of their wives. Whether one or both work, the purpose is mutual benefit for the marital partnership. When there are children, there are shared responsibilities.

Like a knife that descends to sever a cord, this relationship is irrevocably cut off by death. The responsibilities continue--life must go on; jobs must be continued; children at home need attention--but there seems to be little or no meaning to these tasks anymore.

The same loss of meaning extends to special times: special holidays, vacations, times spent with family. Nothing seems "good" anymore. It is like sitting down to a favorite meal without being able to savor it.

Anger and guilt are not usually thought of as having a place in grief. But anger is part of the normal reaction to loss. From the time we are infants, we react with anger to being deprived of something that is of value to us. Anger, in fact, may be thought of as the negative side of sorrow. As sorrow expresses the longing to bring the lost loved one back, anger expresses the sense of deprivation which the loss brings.

Anger is characterized by irritability, bitterness, and an impulse to strike out at an object. This is where anger is terribly frustrating to the widow: There is no appropriate object. Anger is a reaction to the removal of a cherished object or person. If there is someone to blame, someone to punish for the removal, the person is satisfied and the anger recedes. But in death there is literally no one to blame, unless it was caused by a deliberate act.

The lack of an object for anger, coupled with society's taboos against expressing hostility during bereavement, makes anger one of the most difficult emotions to deal with in the grief process. Bereaved persons, frightened by the anger they are feeling or unwilling to acknowledge it, may seek to handle their resentment in various ways, most of them unhealthy.

The widow may deny the anger, repressing it and fleeing from it. Sometimes the result of such repression is a physical illness or an emotional depression.

The bereaved person may turn his/her anger upon others. Widows sometimes accuse hospital personnel or doctors of neglecting the patient or in some way contributing to the patient's death.

The widow may turn the anger upon the loved one, irrationally blaming him/her for dying. This blame may be directed toward the loved one's neglect of health, insistence on carrying on work or activities, or relationship with the bereaved. One woman said: "I know this is silly, but I feel terribly resentful toward my husband for dying and leaving me. He had no business leaving me alone."

Frequently God is the target of the anger. The mourner believes that God could have saved his/her loved one from death. Since He did not, the widow may feel strong anger toward God, as if He had caused the partner to die by not preventing the death.

Most destructive, however, is the tendency of the mourner to turn his/her anger inward. Then it is experienced as guilt. This emotion is probably felt more often than anger is. Guilt may take a number of forms.

A widow may spend a great deal of time going over the past and trying to find places where he/she should have done things differently. The mourner may recall the events leading up to the death. He/she may irrationally internalize guilt for not having recognized the symptoms or gotten the loved one to the hospital sooner or in some other way prevented the death. This is a futile exercise. Hindsight is always more accurate than foresight. Also, even if the bereaved person had done everything that could have been done, there is no guarantee that the outcome would have been different.

A widow may also spend time reliving his/her relationship with the deceased, trying to recall every unpleasant incident in the past. He/she may feel guilt over these incidents, blowing them out of proportion.

Such painful remembering may lead to either of these two types of behavior: self-punishing or self-justifying. Self-punishing behavior may include blaming oneself, refusing to eat, withdrawing from others, or becoming ill. Self-justifying behavior may be expressed by showing an unusual amount of sorrow, idealizing the dead person in an unrealistic way, or extending the mourning period far beyond normal limits.

Fear is very much a part of the grief process. There are two kinds of fear. One is the fear of death itself; the other is fear of the future without the loved one.

Fear of death is basic to being human. The human being is the only creature, so far as we know, that can contemplate its own death. Animals may face death, but they cannot conceive of it before it comes.

We have the capacity to face death in advance, but we do not wish to until we are confronted by it—either in ourselves or in others. Most people shrink from considering the possibility of their own deaths. Perhaps one reason for the morbid curiosity shown in a fatal automobile accident or other violent death is the reassurance that this did not (could not?) happen to the onlookers.

Our whole society is geared toward life rather than death. No one wants to see death, talk about it, make preparation for it. So it is all the more painful to be faced with death as it claims a loved one. The widowed person then must face the fact of death and ask: "If this could happen to my loved one, when might it happen to me?"

The fear of death may trigger physical symptoms. Sometimes the widow may even experience the same kind of symptoms that the dead mate had. A woman may have heart palpitations or chest pains after her husband has died of a heart attack. A man may have severe abdominal pains after his wife has died of intestinal cancer.

The bereaved person may have morbid thoughts about death and may dream of dying. There may be physical or psychological illness within the first six months or year after bereavement. Both men and women seem more prone to illness during the grief period. This is understandable. Persons who study stress find that the most stressful event (100 on a scale of 1-100) is the death of a mate. Next in line is divorce, with a score of 73. Although the suffering from divorce and widowhood are quite similar, it is interesting that there is such a gap in the stress factor between these two painful events. It is not surprising, then, that numbers of persons succumb to illness from the stress of the death of a mate.

The second kind of fear deals with the problems of continued existence without the mate. The widow is actually in a state of alarm. Alarm is defined as the reaction to the loss of safety or defenses. When a mate dies, the remaining partner may feel anxiety over the loss of the person on whom he/she depended for so much life support.

A woman, if she has not worked, may be afraid that she cannot care for herself financially and get along "out in the world." She may be afraid to handle business matters. She may find herself afraid to make decisions.

A man may be afraid that he cannot cope with personal matters. He may not know how to run a house, shop for groceries and personal items. He may be very anxious over caring for the children that are left at home. In each case the anxiety is related to the dominant role the dead mate played in the partnership. This all-pervasive anxiety is experienced both as a general fear and as specific fears related to living without the mate. As new situations arise, there may be new fears. At other times the anxiety may be felt as an undefined foreboding about the future.

The longer two persons have lived together and been dependent on each other, the greater will be these fear reactions. The depth of the loss makes it difficult for the survivor to imagine living without the partner. Thus the bereaved person dreads and fears the prospect of living alone, perhaps for years. However, this does not apply simply to longer marriages. Brief marriages, where there has been a strong attachment between the partners, can bring the same dread of a future without the mate.

Old childhood fears, long since laid aside, may resurface during this period of stress. Such reappearances are probably connected with the sense of alarm and loss of safety. When persons feel generally secure, phobias and other outgrown fears tend to be minimized. But at a time of stress and defenselessness, the old fears become active again.

Loneliness is a reaction that often increases during the months of bereavement, rather than decreasing. At first the widow may have much support from friends and relatives. But soon these persons turn to their own activities again, leaving the mourner essentially alone. The sense of abandonment, both by the dead and by the living, then becomes acute.

Loneliness is especially difficult for people who have been married for a long time.

Many of these went directly from the parental roof to the marital roof, with perhaps a short stay in a college dormitory or a military barracks. They have had no experience of living alone. For them suddenly to be plunged into aloneness is both frightening and painful.

Also, most married couples are used to having a built-in support system. They do not know how to reach out to others and make friends "on their own." Men often leave the "social side" of their lives to their wives. Women, too, have problems. They are used to making friends by pairs. They find themselves left out of many gatherings because they have no escort. Neither male nor female widows have many friendship skills that would help them to establish new relationships or to reconstruct old friendships as single persons.

As a result, many widowed persons stay at home, lonely and bitter over the loss of their married friends. If men date, they follow the patterns set in their adolescent dating days. Women look for men to take them out, afraid to venture on their own.

It is true that most couples tend to desert their widowed friends. If the friendships have been purely on a couples basis, the loss of one part in the foursome may break up the friendship entirely. Even if it does not, there is a sense of discomfort among the remaining parties. Couple friendships in general do not survive the loss of one party.

Depression is a painful state, fairly common but not very well understood. Unlike some of the other reactions, it is not an expression of a specific emotion. It is the absence of emotion and of physical and mental energy.

Depression is characterized by a sense of futility and worthlessness. Persons with this reaction are persistently gloomy and pessimistic. They are self-preoccupied, blaming and depreciating themselves. Physical energy is so low that the bereaved person may have difficulty getting out of bed and getting started. He/she may experience difficulty in concentrating and in thinking clearly. Severe insomnia, with early morning waking, may add to the lack of energy. Sometimes there is loss of appetite.

Connected with these symptoms are physical complaints, such as headache, back pains, palpitations, and constipation. The depressed person may think he/she has some physical illness, and such a fear will add to the depression.

During this time it is hard to express emotions, even weeping. The person may give in to despair to the point of entertaining ideas of suicide.

This state may occur at different stages in the grief process. Sometimes it will occur almost immediately, especially if the mourner experiences emotions that he/she cannot cope with. Depression may come on gradually. The mourner may get into the state without realizing what has happened. Depression may even come after apparent recovery from grief.

It is not clear what causes depression. It seems to be connected with inability to deal with the emotions felt in grief. For instance, the reaction of hostility may have been turned inward as guilt. If the mourner finds it too difficult to deal with the guilt and hostility, depression may result. Or the bereaved person may be so gripped by fear or loneliness that he/she may retreat into depression.

This state may last a few weeks or several months, but it usually disappears. In cases of severe depression, drugs may be prescribed by a physician to handle some of the symptoms. But the recovery generally is related to working through the repressed emotions or to a renewed interest in living.

Depression may be seen as the personality's way of dealing with frustration or too much emotion. In this way depression may be compared to shock as a defense. When the personality recovers the ability to deal with the emotions or the frustration, the symptoms of depression gradually disappear.

Acceptance is the final reaction to death. This is the stage when the person's emotions at last accept what the person's mind has known all the time: The loved one is gone forever and will not return.

Acceptance is expressed both as *resignation* and *peace*. With these emotions acceptance becomes a bridging stage. Resignation is the final reaction of grief. Peace is the first reaction of new life. Some widows stop with resignation. They are resigned to their loss, but they continue to live in the shadow of it. But those who find true peace are the ones who move on to the emotions of renewed life.

With peace, grief work comes to an end. The widow has worked through his/her attachment to the dead mate and is now willing to put it in the past. Now the widow is ready to move on to a life beyond death. This "new life" will include new roles, new friendships, new activities. Its main characteristic is that the person is again able to enjoy life, to experience pleasure in living without shame or guilt. He/she is again at peace and looking toward the future, not the past.

The emotions beyond grief are hope, love, and joy. Persons who have passed through bereavement and come to acceptance are in a position to experience these emotions to the full.

Hope is the emotion related to the future. The widow may consider the years ahead with new hope. This does not mean that all problems have vanished. But there are also new possibilities. The person on the other side of grief is ready to consider these opportunities. He/she can hope to make a full life.

Love is again possible to the widow. Loving relationships need not be narrowly constricted to the idea of marrying again, although that is now a healthy possibility. The widow is ready to live in the present, not the past. Therefore, he/she is open to marriage. Love, however, can be expressed in many ways to many people: to children and grandchildren, to old friends, to new friends and acquaintances, to persons in need.

Joy comes with hope and love. It is a deep happiness that wells out of the inner life of a person. Those who have lived through the dark shadows of death and walked in the deep valleys of sorrow can better appreciate joy. They have lived with death. Therefore, they can celebrate life. This celebration takes the form of joy.

Only those, perhaps, who have known death intimately can appreciate life fully. It is the purpose of grief work to bring such persons to the place where they can exchange the garments of mourning for the raiment of joy.

2
Grief Work—
Early Stages

Grief is not only a set of emotions. It is a process, a period of time in which the mourner seeks to come to terms emotionally with the fact of death. The mourner knows at once, intellectually, that the loved person has died. But knowing this in the emotions and accepting it, so that life may go on, takes much longer. During this process the mourner needs to accomplish some very important tasks.

1. Deal with the emotions of grief.
2. Put the relationship with the dead spouse in perspective as an important part of the past.
3. Redefine roles and relationships with family and friends and in society.
4. Affirm one's right to live in the present and the future without the dead loved one.

These goals are not easy to achieve. For this reason it is appropriate to call the grief process "grief work." It takes real work to move through the stages of grief and come out a whole person, ready to take up life again fully.

The major task is to deal with the loss of the relationship with the dead loved one. The pain of losing that relationship calls forth the emotions of grief. These must be dealt with, not ignored or explained away.

It is important to put the relationship with the dead person in the past. A living person cannot continue to sustain a relationship with a dead person without remaining in death, also. This may sound like a harsh judgment. But it is absolutely necessary for ongoing, healthy life. The deceased person has ceased to live. There is no change, no growth for that person in the earthly life. At whatever age he/she died, the dead person will be remembered as being at that point. If the spouse lives thirty more years, the dead partner will be remembered as being thirty years younger! The living person needs to grow, to change. By holding on to a static relationship, the living may cease to grow. Or he/she may be afraid to venture into new ways of living.

It is not uncommon to hear widowed persons speak as if their dead spouses were still involved in their lives and decisions. Such persons may say, "What would my husband/wife want me to do about this?" or, "I could't do that! My husband/wife wouldn't want me to."

Such statements are unrealistic. Conditions change. What the dead loved one would have wanted probably fit the situation when he/she died. But with new conditions the spouse, if alive, likely would have had much different opinions.

As the relationship with the dead spouse is gradually put in the past, there is the need to redefine roles and relationships. Roles in our society are often determined by marital status. The widowed person has to stop thinking of himself/herself as a spouse and begin to think as a single person. Relationships also change. These may be relationships with children, as a parent assumes the roles of both father and mother. There may be new relationships with the family of the deceased spouse. Relationships with married friends also change. The widow may find himself/herself more comfortable with single persons, at least for a time.

Finally, putting the relationship with the dead person in the past releases the widow from dependence on the former partner.

The life that was shared is now over. But there is still life for the bereaved person. When the grief work has been completed, the widowed person can take up life again in a new sense. This life will have been enriched by the former relationship. When two people have lived together as one, each has given much to the other. These gifts remain. They can be reinvested in the life of the widow. Also, grief gives a new dimension to life. Only those who have lived arduously and triumphantly through grief know what new strengths and inner resources they now possess for meeting the worst—and the best—that life can offer.

Because the major task is dealing with the relationship that has been terminated by death, the stages of grief work are stated with regard to this relationship. I have defined four stages, from my study and experience: living with the dead; living without the dead; living for the dead; and living beyond death.

Where there is a long terminal illness, some of the tasks and emotions of grief may be faced before the death of the spouse. These reactions are called "anticipatory grief." Grieving actually begins when there is a realization that the loved one is probably going to die. Sometimes, in cases of painful and prolonged illness, much of the work of grief is done by the time the actual death occurs. I have identified two stages of anticipatory grief: living with the dying and living through death.

Let us consider the stages of grief in order, beginning with anticipatory grief.

Living with the Dying

Moving through the stages of approaching death with a loved one is very different from facing a sudden or unexpected death. The husband-wife relationship is probably the closest one human beings know. This closeness is demonstrated as the well person feels many of the reactions of the dying person.

Myron Madden, in his book *Raise the Dead!*, has suggested some progressive phases through which both the dying person and the well person move toward death. They are:

"Impossible"—This can't be happening to us.

"Possible"—This may be happening.

"Impending"—This is happening.

"Fact"—This (death) has occurred.[1]

In her definitive book *On Death and Dy-*

ing, Elisabeth Kubler-Ross spells out reactions that belong to each of these phases. They are:

"Denial and Isolation" (*Impossible* phase)

"Anger" and "Bargaining" (*Possible* phase)

"Depression" and "Acceptance" (*Impending* phase).

Kubler-Ross has stated these reactions in terms of the dying person. However, she notes that "family members undergo different stages of adjustment similar to the ones described for our patients."[2]

Persons who experience these reactions deal, to some extent, with all the emotions of grief. They gradually "let go" of their loved one as the disease progresses. And they have to begin to redefine their roles and relationships. If there are children at home, the well parent must begin to take on the tasks of both parents. The well person begins to have the experience of going places alone and of being alone at home a good deal of the time. This is the case if the sick person is in a hospital. If he/she is being cared for at home, the well person will be confined. Relationships with the outside world will be effectually cut off, to some extent at least.

By the time the actual death occurs, therefore, the well person has done a lot of his/her grief work. This is one reason why persons widowed by a terminal illness tend to recover from their grief fairly quickly.

It is said that there is a timetable for grief. A certain length of time—which is different for each person—is needed to work through the stages and emotions of grief. As has been said, grieving begins with death or when the inevitability of death is perceived. So after a terminal illness, the widowed person has done a great deal of grieving before the time of the actual death.

Let us look at the phases of dying and the emotions connected with them.

Impossible.—The shock of learning that a spouse probably will die is traumatic. The very word *terminal* carries a psychological shock. So do the words *critical, cancer, heart attack,* and *stroke.* All these carry the connotation of possible death.

Denial accompanies the shock. It is impossible to take in the possibility of death. This is especially true when the spouse is still alive. No matter how sick he/she may be, our tendency is to believe that the person can be made well. This tendency is important to maintain. In the early stages of illness, it can well make the difference between life and death. However, denial can be maintained far beyond healthy limits. Some family members hold on to their denial of the seriousness of the illness long after that position is realistic. Some persons stubbornly refuse to recognize the signs of impending death: a weakening body, evidences of deterioration from disease, lack of response to treatment, bodily changes that are irreversible.

The isolation that comes with such prolonged denial is often extreme. The patients and their families do not want to hear unpleasant truths from their doctors. They shut themselves away from their medical helpers, their friends, and one another. My mother used to have a saying about illness: "Ignore it, and it will go away." All too many people, faced with the prognosis of possible death, seem to adopt this philosophy.

Possible.—As shock drains off, anger takes its place. Both patient and the spouse begin to ask why. Why should this disease have come? Why should it be fatal? Why can't the doctors do more? Why doesn't God answer prayers for healing?

Before death, anger becomes a way of fighting back. Often both patient and spouse pour much of their energies into attacks on doctors and nurses, on other family members, on God, or on each other.

Anger may give rise to guilt. The spouse may feel responsible for the sick one's illness. He/she may feel that not enough precautions were taken. Perhaps the patient should have been forced to get medical attention earlier. All such thoughts may trouble the mind of the spouse.

The "guilty" person may engage in bargaining—with God, with the doctors, or with the sick spouse. The well person will make all kinds of promises; to give the patient the very best of care if she/he can go home; to follow the doctor's orders to the letter; to be more faithful to God and the church; to begin the practice of tithing or some other new commitment; to be a better wife/husband to the sick spouse. All these promises have one underlying purpose—to strike a bargain with somebody so that the spouse will not die.

Bargaining also may be a way of buying time. If the spouse cannot get well, at least his/her life may be prolonged. Promises may be made, or bargains suggested, that would prolong life, if not restore health. The sick spouse is urged to "hang on" until a child graduates, until the couple can take a trip, or until an anniversary can be celebrated. These are all delaying tactics.

In this stage fear is beginning to be felt openly. During periods of shock and anger, the underlying fear may not be evident. But the fear of death and of living without the loved one is a constant ingredient of life for the well person. Fear fuels the sense of desperation in bargaining. Fear, also, can cause accusations that not enough is being done to heal the patient.

Impending.—In this stage both patient and spouse face the almost certain fact that death will occur. The patient may experience depression. This is not the usual depression, such as described in the previous chapter. Kubler-Ross calls it a "preparatory depression." For the dying person it is a time of quiet sorrow and resignation. It is the time when the patient begins to say good-bye to all that he/she holds dear in life.

The spouse may also be feeling depression. But this likely will be more like the normal depression. This term describes a time of depressing the emotions. It usually results from too much expenditure of emotional and physical energy. Or it may come from repressing emotions, not allowing them to be felt or expressed.

During this period the spouse may have been feeling a number of emotions. There may be increasing loneliness. If the ill spouse is confined to a hospital, the well spouse will be much alone. Also, there are changing roles. The spouse is having to take over many of the duties of the marital partnership which were formerly borne by the sick person.

There will be more apparent fear. The well spouse is facing the reality of approaching death. All of us fear death; few of us want to face it. For the spouse there is the fear of the future: What will it be like to live without the beloved? It is not surprising that sometimes, after long and close companionship, the death of the surviving spouse follows shortly upon the death of the first partner.

Sorrow now is more open. Previously the spouse may have wept secretly. Or he/she may have believed that such tears were a betrayal of hope. Now he/she may express these feelings more openly.

However, the well spouse may suppress

these feelings for various reasons. He/she may feel the necessity to "be strong" for the sake of the dying person. There may be a "conspiracy of silence," so that husband and wife conceal from each other their knowledge of the true situation. Well-meaning family members may be hanging on to hope. To express sorrow may seem to them to be giving up hope. But if the spouse cannot express some of these feelings of loneliness, fear, and sorrow, the grieving process after death will be more painful and prolonged. Emotions need to be acknowledged and expressed, even though some limits must be placed on such expression.

Therefore, the depression felt by the spouse may be akin to the way depression is felt in the grief period following death. There will, however, be some elements of resignation in the depression. It is impossible to spend hours by the bedside of a sick person without some knowledge of what is happening. As they yield to the reaction of depression, both husband and wife can be more honest about their impending separation. If this can be done, both partners may move to the point of acceptance.

This reaction is one of accepting the inevitable. Christians often find this time one of real victory over death. Acceptance can be more than blind resignation. It is a recognition that death is not the end of life but only the door to true life. If death is approached with this attitude, the pain of parting will be partly eased. Along with sorrow there will be mingled emotions of hope, peace, joy, faith, and courage.

Often, because of the nature of the illness and the widespread use of sedatives, the patient may not be lucid enough to talk much about the impending departure. But honesty and openness at this time are very important on both sides.

Living Through Death

In past centuries most people died at home, unless they died a violent death. They were lucid, though often in pain, at the time of death. Their loved ones generally were by the bedside. So most people went through the stage of "living through death." They were present when death occurred.

Persons now, for the most part, die in hospitals or nursing homes. The recent growth of the hospice movement is an attempt to return the act of dying to the home or a homelike setting. Sometimes the family is not notified of the imminence of death. The death may come so suddenly that notice cannot be given. Or the patient may be in an intensive-care unit, where family members cannot be admitted in a group. All these circumstances make it rather unusual for the family to participate in the last moments of their loved ones. The stage of "living through death" is therefore not commonly experienced. Even when there is a terminal illness, the family may not know of the death until after it has occurred.

But for those who are present with their dying loved ones, this stage is a very definite one. The situation may vary from the patient being very lucid to being in a coma. The spouse may be either ready to participate in this event, or he/she may be emotionally unable to do much except be present.

There are, however, certain definite consequences of passing through this stage. It marks the passing from life to death. Death is the great divider. No matter how long a person has been ill, no matter how much the approaching death has been anticipated, no one can really be prepared for it. Dying is like walking through a door which then closes irrevocably. The living person is left on this side. The pain of separation is clear and keen. What was once a living, breathing person is now an empty shell. To be present at this event means that death must be faced. This is the first important step in the process of grief.

"Living through death" may help to conquer the fear of death which is in all of us. It can be seen as a natural event, a movement from one sphere of life to another.

This stage also gives opportunity to communicate with the loved one about love, grief, hope for the opportunity to meet again, and peace as both face their separation. There can be a chance to express thankfulness for the years together. Most important, there is the opportunity to say good-bye. This event has the same effect as the good-bye rituals we perform when we go to airports, railroad stations, and bus depots to say our good-byes. We want to emphasize the importance of our relationship with departing friends or relatives by being present when they leave. "Saying good-bye" fulfills a human craving to seal relationships when persons will not meet again, at least for a period of time. How much more important it is to say good-bye when a loved one takes his/her last earthly journey!

Saying good-bye on both sides is only possible when the sick person is able to communicate. But being present still has the force of a "letting-go" ritual. and it gives the surviving partner a definite memory of the time of separation. This memory is important in beginning to get hold of what has happened. We can be told that someone close to us has died, and intellectually we understand that fact. But we need many kinds of reinforcing experiences to bring that fact home emotionally.

The period immediately after death may include both reinforcing and denying experiences. Much of the funeral ritual is ambivalent in this regard. Persons come to "pay their respects" to the dead. But in doing so, they try to avoid talking about death. They will speak of the departed person as if he/she were still alive. The arts of the funeral director serve to make the dead person look alive, so far as possible.

At the same time, the funeral itself is generally a realistic ceremony emphasizing the fact that this person is no longer living. Hymns, Scripture readings, prayers, and eulogies center around the fact of death and the hope of eternal life. The interment of the body vividly pictures the separation which death brings.

Ambivalence is present even in these ceremonies, however. The word "death" is often avoided. And increasingly there is a tendency to bypass the interment ceremony.

With all its ambivalence, the ritual of the funeral and the mourning period that precedes it provide important helps to the widowed person and the bereaved family. It gives a structured time and procedure for mourning. Both family and friends know what is expected of them during this period. It also provides opportunity to center attention on the lost loved one. Everyone may talk about him/her at length, without the embarrassment that might be felt in other settings. And the funeral service itself is a source of great comfort. The resources built up by these events generally give the widowed person the strength to begin the tasks of grief work, beginning with the first stage of grief after death.

Living with the Dead

The first reaction to death is shock. This is true even when there has been preparation for the death. It is more acute, of course, where the death is unexpected. As the widow tries to adjust to the shock of death, he/she may find that it is difficult to think of the mate as dead. In the widow's mind, the mate is still alive but inaccessible.

So, for a period of days or perhaps weeks, the widow may experience the mate as still alive "somewhere." He/she may fantasize the mate as being away, as still in the hospital, or as in some other room of the house. The mate may seem to be very near and present in spirit. Some widows report hearing the mate speaking to them internally. They may even have the illusion of seeing the mate fleetingly. These are not in any way evidences of an unbalanced mind. They are ways the person uses emotions to begin to adjust to the fact that the mate is indeed gone and is inaccessible.

Many people dream vividly of the dead person (as being alive) in these first weeks. These dreams may be painful or joyful. But the awakening, to realize again the loss, is always sorrowful.

All these experiences are part of "living with the dead." The living mate is still not emotionally ready to accept the death of his/her loved one. The mourner deeply desires to recapture the presence of the lost person. It is as if he/she were searching for the dead person, in the same way as one would search for someone who was physically lost.

Moving through this first stage can be inhibited if the mourner refuses to deal with the actuality of the death. Keeping the dead person's clothes and possessions intact and in their accustomed places, visiting the grave daily, and speaking of the dead as if he/she were still alive are all devices to avoid the pain of reality. The cost of these devices is steep in the long run. Death is death, and it is final. To continue to hold on to the dead person is, in effect, a way of dying oneself. The significant fact about the loved one now is that he/she is dead. The person who clings to a dead body is not living. He/she is existing in a state of death.

Another unhealthy way of dealing with this stage is to avoid it altogether. Some persons try to blot out all thoughts of the dead mate. They avoid persons and situations that would remind them of their loss. They may plunge feverishly into a hectic round of activities that give them little time for reflection.

They may even form a premature attachment to someone new. Or they may display an intense devotion to a new interest. Such a turning outward is good when it comes at the right time in the grief process. But in the early stages of bereavement, such attachments inhibit grief work. Then both the person and his/her new attachments may suffer deeply.

This first stage is very difficult for most people because it is so foreign to the way most of us live. We avoid thoughts of death or dead persons. But it is necessary to confront one's feelings and reactions at this time. Only by doing so can the personality cope gradually with the fact that the loved companion has gone from the earthly scene.

As the reality of the death becomes clearer, there will be waves of sorrow that seem almost to engulf the mourner. These waves of sorrow generally mark the transition from "living with the dead" to the intermediate stages.

3
Grief Work—
Intermediate Stages

The intermediate stages of grief last much longer than the first stage. Both "living without the dead" and "living for the dead" may be experienced at the same time. They seem to weave in and out as reactions to the loss of the loved one. "Living without the dead" seems to be more common and more readily recognized. So it will be considered first.

Living Without the Dead

This stage of grief is much longer than "living with the dead." In fact, for numbers of widows, it becomes a way of life. There are persons who have never ceased to mourn the dead. They shape their whole lives in the consciousness of their loss.

This sense of loss is predominant throughout this stage. The dead person is thought of less in the present. The widow's preoccupations are with the dead mate in the past. And the future without the mate becomes an obsession. How can I live without my husband (my wife)? is the spoken or unspoken question.

Emotions in This Stage

Sorrow is very deeply felt. But it is not so constant as in the first weeks. It comes in waves and then subsides. The widow finds the sorrow difficult to control. Throughout all this period (which may last several months or a year or more), pangs of sorrow may clutch at the mourner. These may come when they are least expected. Often a wave of sorrow sweeps over the widow as he/she is unexpectedly reminded of the dead person. Other reactions, such as fear or loneliness, may bring on weeping and anguish.

It is important to let sorrow flow. Often persons—men especially—do not have inward permission to let the sorrow out. People in Western cultures look with astonishment at the Eastern peoples who weep and sob without any seeming control. But we would do well to take lessons from them. Sorrow is the proper reaction to a severe loss, and it needs to be expressed.

Also, sorrow is most helpfully expressed

when it can be let out in the presence of loving and understanding friends. Unfortunately, this is not always possible. There are
many taboos against such expressions. But
the widow who can find such a friend will
discover that this stage of deep sorrow
passes more quickly.

During this period, especially at first,
holidays and anniversaries are quite painful. Then, particularly at Thanksgiving and
Christmas, the loss is most evident. The
empty chair at the table is all too plain! The
birthday of the mate, the wedding anniversary, and the anniversary of the mate's
death are all painful occasions. Other special days in the family may arouse sad
memories.

Different people respond to such occasions differently. Some may try to deny the
sadness, throwing themselves into being
happy "for the family." Others may refuse
to celebrate at all.

It is important to realize that these occasions will become less painful as the years
pass. The first time is usually the hardest.
Allowing oneself to feel sorrow and to allow
others the same privilege can be very healing. Our tradition of family holidays, such
as "home for Christmas," has its beauty but

also its desolation. The more meaningful a family holiday has been, the more pain will be involved in celebrating it without the dead family member.

Part of putting the relationship with the dead spouse in the past is involved with these holidays. It is all right to recognize the loss when the holidays are celebrated for the first time or two. But the widow can give himself/herself permission to change these traditions. Holidays can be made meaningful in ways that are different from the time when the mate was alive.

Loneliness becomes a very real factor, as soon as the initial support from relatives and friends begins to be withdrawn. Our mourning period is so brief that bereaved persons are tacitly expected to "get back in the swim" within a very short time after the funeral. Visits and calls from friends may continue for a time longer, as will invitations to meals. But within about a month, usually, these drop to a minimum. It is then that the mourner begins to feel the chill of isolation from companionship.

A woman, who had been widowed two months, called me in great distress to say that all of her friends had deserted her. For the past three years she had taken care of her terminally ill husband day and night. She had refused all invitations. She had even discouraged friends from coming to the home because her husband did not feel comfortable with them. Now she was alone and lonely, needing the companionship she had had to refuse earlier.

This sense of isolation carries over into activities that the widow previously enjoyed as part of a couple. Men sometimes quit going to church because they do not have a wife to sit with. It is too painful to sit alone and be reminded of their loss. A man told me with anguish of going to a picnic given by the men of the church to which the wives were invited. He went alone. He said that his friends greeted him warmly. But at mealtime all the couples went off, and he was left alone. He did not know how to invite himself to join a couple, and so he ate by himself.

I have heard many women say with anger that they are no longer welcomed by their married women friends because the wives "see us as a threat." I do not believe that this is true. Much of it is a projection by the widowed women. They do not understand why they are isolated, and they search for reasons.

In many cases the true reason is that the wives feel uncomfortable in the presence of their widowed friend. They do not know what to say to her. Any topic of conversation may seem to flaunt their marriedness against her widowhood. The threat is not that of the widow tempting the husband. The real threat is more insidious: it is the threat of death. If this can happen to our friend, who can say whether it may happen to us—or when? We all shrink from death or the reminders of death.

Loneliness, either in a crowd or when alone, is painful. For most people the empty house is a constant reminder of the loss. Men especially find it hard to come home in the evening to emptiness. Women are often most lonely at night, going to bed in an empty house. Even the presence of children does not totally alleviate the loneliness. The children and their needs are only poignant reminders of the lost mate.

Another problem with loneliness is that most married people have long since lost the skills of making friends as individuals. The world, a single person has said wryly, is like Noah's ark: everyone goes two by two. Many people marry either out of high school or out of college. The friendliness skills appropriate to those ages usually revolved around dating and school social affairs. Those skills are of little use now.

One of the tasks in working through this stage of grief is to learn to make friends on a single basis. Fortunately, we are beginning to have more help in this area. Singles' groups sponsored by churches or other community agencies offer places to learn and practice friend-making skills. It is not necessary to repeat adolescent dating patterns in order to have friends. Adults can have friends among persons of both sexes with similar interests and ideals. It can be exciting to learn to make friends of different ages and different life-styles, so long as these persons are compatible in their ideals and interests.

It takes time to begin to be independent and interdependent. Widows have to handle their lives on their own. At the same time, they need to reach out to sources of help beyond themselves and their own families. Some of the sources of help which they found in their mates are available from friends and from skilled workers. A widowed woman, for instance, can find a trusted mechanic to care for her car. A widowed man can look to a schoolteacher for help and advice in dealing with his teenage daughter.

Before this task can be worked through, however, there will be many painful moments. These times are often characterized by *fear*. Being without emotional and physical support is felt by the personality as a threat. This threat triggers fear.

In our culture, probably, men's loneliness is more often recognized than women's. And women's fears are probably recognized more than men's. And so men are often invited out to meals, while women are urged to get a dog: "It'll be company for you, and also give you protection."

Fears of various kinds are outlined in the chapter on emotions. There are several constructive ways to handle fears. One is to recognize the fear without trying to repress it. Another is to separate the reality in the fear from imaginary components. It is realistic to fear getting sick while alone, without someone in the house to call on. It is unrealistic to allow that fear to prey on the mind to the point that every slight symptom is blown out of proportion.

A most important procedure in dealing with fear is to handle its realistic aspects so that these are overcome or at least minimized. The person who is afraid of falling ill alone may build up a support system of friends and neighbors. He/she may ask neighbors to watch for signs of activity around the house. Arrangements may be made with friends to make phone calls at certain times. When the realistic part of the fear has been dealt with, the widow can then devote his/her energies to dealing with the fear itself.

There are good ways of handling fear: calling a friend just to talk when the fear rises; reading a relaxing book or watching a television program to get one's mind off the fear; reciting a favorite Bible verse about trusting God; praying. Most fears come when the widow is alone, and often in the wakeful night hours. Coping with fears is a part of learning to live alone without the mate. And finding ways to handle fears will lead to more confidence in living alone.

Another reaction to the deprivation of the widow's support system is *anger.* This emotion is often taboo to persons who have been raised by Christian principles. But anger is a vital part of life. Without anger we could not protect ourselves or deal with injustice in the world.

Part of anger is involved in asking why.

This is a totally legitimate question. We have been asking why from early childhood. In fact, the ability to ask why is a part of being human. But it is also important to recognize that *why* does not always have an answer.

We have already looked at the forms anger takes and the unhealthy ways persons often deal with it. These are steps in dealing with anger as a healthy method:

1. Recognize the anger for what it is. Don't try to hide it or deny it. Affirm your right to be angry in this situation. Remember that God Himself put the capacity for anger within the human personality. Affirm to yourself that God accepts you with your anger. He is not disturbed by it, even if it should be directed at Him.

2. Find ways to ventilate the energy generated by the anger. Do housecleaning, gardening, or carpentry work. Jog, swim, or engage in any kind of sport that releases energy without arousing tension. Walk fast if that is the only kind of exercise you are capable of. Then give yourself a chance to relax.

3. Find persons with whom you can vent your anger. These should be friends who will listen to your feelings without getting

emotionally involved themselves. If you don't have such friends or don't feel comfortable exploding in front of them, look for a person trained to deal with emotions. This may be a counselor in a church or a family counseling center. But it is important to open up the anger and express it.

You may have to go through these three steps several times. Anger will subside and then rise again. But if it is dealt with in a healthy manner, the feeling will eventually begin to disappear. And it will not go underground into guilt toward yourself or out in hostility toward other people.

In the midst of dealing with all these emotions, it is important for the widow not to make major decisions. So much mental and emotional energy go into sorrow, fear, anger, and loneliness that the widow does not have enough left over to deal with decision-making. Also, in this stage the person's mind is not as clear as it will be later on.

Unfortunately, well-meaning friends and family members may urge decisions on the widow at this time: to sell the home and move to an apartment or to move in with one of the children; to get a job or to change jobs; to take a long trip; to get married again.

No such major decisions should be made during the early part of this stage unless they are absolutely necessary. This is the time for "centering in." It is the time for dealing with what is going on inside the person, rather than handling too many outward details.

Redefining Roles

There is a profound change in role for the widow, especially for the woman. The widowed woman may have difficulty finding her place in our society. She may lose her status, which often has been based on her husband's name and his position in society. When there is no longer a husband, status is lost. Women feel this loss keenly, whether they state it in these terms or not.

Some women try to carry on some status through retaining their husband's names on charge accounts, bank accounts, and telephone listings. At one time some of this was necessary, especially in charge accounts. Fortunately this situation is changing rapidly. Widowed women can get credit in their own names.

Even if such changes are made, the widow probably will not want to do so at first. The use of the husband's name is familiar and comfortable. Unless she has a profession which makes it easy for her to take her own name, she may prefer to continue using her husband's name. The trap here, however, is that she continues to take her status from the dead person. In many cases it can be healthy to revert to a woman's given name rather than continuing to carry her dead husband's name.

The problem is more with the role than with the status. The widow in our society who does not have a profession really has no role. Someone has said, "We don't bury our widows alive; we just ignore them." A woman who has had a full life with a clearly defined role as a wife suddenly finds herself without this role. It takes time to work through this void and find a new role. Such a role needs to be based on what the woman is as an individual, not on society's expectations of her.

The widowed man suffers from role loss, also, but in a different way. His status is not lost, for the man takes his status from his work. But often his sense of self-importance is badly damaged. For many men, their work does not provide much status. But a man can look upon it as a means of providing for his family. So he defines his worth in terms of what his daily toil does for his family. He is a "good provider." With the loss of his wife, unless there are children still at home, his role as provider is gone. So is much of his worth in his own eyes.

If there are children at home, there is still a role change. Instead of losing a role, he has added one. He is already father/provider. Now he must be also mother/sustainer. The added role can be a heavy strain on men who have not had to deal with this side of family life.

The same problem applies to the woman with children at home. Unless she is left well-provided for (which is unlikely), she has to add father/provider to her role as mother/sustainer. This can be a heavy strain on her mental, physical, and emotional resources.

For both the widowed father and the widowed mother, it is important to recognize one's limitations. The father cannot totally be mother. The mother cannot totally be father. But single parents can look for father-substitutes or mother-substitutes to help them with the role-modeling and parenting that their children need. Coaches, schoolteachers, church workers with youth and children, friends, and relatives all may play a part in giving the children of one sur-viving parent rich experiences such as the deceased parent would have given them.

Being a husband or wife is basically a sex-ual role. Therefore the widow is faced with the problem of sexual fulfillment. Women may be harassed by "helpful" male friends—sometimes even husbands of their women friends. These men want to "help" relieve the widow's sexual frustrations. Sometimes the woman is emotionally dev-astated by such suggestions. Or she may give in, either for casual sex or for an affair. Such experiences, since they do not involve commitment or permanence, may leave her in worse shape emotionally than before.

Men, too, have problems. In the singles world they may encounter women who are eager for affairs. The temptation is great for men to engage in such casual encounters. But the result for them, as for the women, may be more loneliness, isolation, and emo-tional frustration.

For both widowed men and women such affairs can be self-destructive. What these people are looking for is the companionship they have lost, of which sexual relationships are the major expression. A one-night stand or a short-term affair does nothing to restore that companionship.

In spite of the frustrations, sexual chastity is important for the widowed person. As long as the grief process is going on, he/she does not have the emotional balance to sustain a deep relationship with a person of the opposite sex. When the widow is no longer seeking to restore the lost relationship, he/she is ready to find a new relationship.

Early marriage is a trap for sexually frustrated persons, especially men. Probably the reason why so many men marry women who remind them of their dead wives, or who were close friends of their wives, is their unconscious desire to recreate the former relationship. Many such marriages succeed, if the man has had long enough to begin to establish himself as a separate person from his dead wife. But premature marriages often end in divorce. Then the man's loss of self-esteem is great, and his ability to form a satisfying marital relationship is impaired.

For all these reasons, it is important for the widow to redefine his/her role as part of the process of leaving the dead past behind.

Redefinition of roles comes as the person finds new ways of relating to persons around him/her. Taking a job will give a woman who has not had a job a new role and a different status. Finding new friends, on an individual rather than a couple basis, can help the widow of either sex to have a new role. Getting involved in helping groups, hobby clubs, and civic or religious organizations assists the widow in finding new and satisfying roles. These will be based on individual accomplishment rather than on marital condition.

Even while the widow is coping with "living without the dead," he/she is still attached emotionally to the partner by trying, consciously or unconsciously, to keep that partnership alive. This stage of grief work is called "living for the dead."

Living for the Dead

In one sense "living for the dead" is a separate stage of grief, because it is a different way of relating to the departed mate. In another sense this is an unhealthy attempt to avoid working through the stage of living without the dead. By living for the dead the widow perpetuates the life of the dead mate. But the cost to the widow may be his/her own life. Living for the dead saps the vital energy that should be used to recover one's own life.

It is a way of denying the death of the mate. It is also an attempt to find meaning in life by carrying on the work or fulfilling the wishes of the dead person. It may be an unconscious attempt to assuage guilt which the living person may feel because he/she is alive while the mate is dead. Or there may be guilt over past failures in the relationship.

These are some of the reasons why persons trap themselves into living for the dead:

1. A desire to hold on to the dead mate;

2. A way to continue the shared identity known in the marital relationship;

3. Pressure exerted by the mate before death for the surviving member to continue his/her life through carrying out the dead person's wishes;

4. A desire to keep one's identity intact by being related to the dead person's work; and

5. A desire to relieve guilt feelings.

Ways of Living for the Dead

The bereaved person may live for the dead in a variety of ways.

1. *Assuming an unfinished task left by the dead.*—Perhaps the dead person was in

the midst of a project which meant a lot to him. His widow may seek to complete the project, trying to enlist the aid of his friends or business associates. She may even try to do it more perfectly than her husband would have.

2. *Carrying on the work of the dead as if he were doing it.*—This often occurs where the dead person has had his own business or has been in a political office. His widow will take over for her dead husband. This is often a good thing to do. What makes it unhealthy is for the widow, when "living for the dead," to subordinate all her ideas. She will seek to do her dead husband's work just as he would have done.

This desire may be unrealistic. It does not take into account changing circumstances. Death is static; time stands still for the dead. But life is dynamic. What might have been realistic in the lifetime of the dead person may become impossible. So it can be very frustrating to a woman to try to carry on her husband's work as he would have done it when he was alive. The truth is that if he were alive, he probably would have been making changes in the light of changing conditions. Trying to follow the "lead" of the dead means to ignore the dynamic changes of life.

3. *Carrying out the wishes of the dead person about rearing children, keeping the house as it had been, and so on.*—When a woman dies leaving children, she may impose her desires for her children and her home upon her husband. She may do this explicitly or implicitly.

The widow who "lives for the dead" may seek to carry out these wishes rigidly with his children. But the same problem applies as in carrying on the dead man's work. Children change as they grow. Treating them just as their mother wished before her death can become very unrealistic. This static kind of expectation can breed resentment and rebellion in the children. Furthermore, there is no guarantee that she would not have changed in her dealings with the children if she had been alive.

4. *Refusing to marry.*—Sometimes the living partner will determine never to remarry. This decision may come from an expressed desire of the dead person. Or it may be the widow's determination to "live for the dead" by continuing to be the spouse of the dead for the rest of his/her life.

It is not always possible to remarry, of course. But it can be unhealthy to make a fixed decision never to do so, especially if it is for the sake of the dead partner. Life goes on. Part of the dynamic in life is tied up with close relationships, particularly marriage.

All these examples show unhealthiness by ignoring the dynamic character of life. The person who tried to take the place of the dead in life, and thus perpetuate the dead person's life, is losing his/her own life. Myron Madden has some insightful statements on this situation:

> When we insist on 'keeping faith' with the dead by not accepting their death, we deprive ourselves of the very process which restores our loss so that our life can be reinvested. . . .
>
> We cannot remain with the dead: where we try to make this happen death and life get mixed in a strange way so that the living person comes to absorb the dead person.[1]

Emotions in This Stage

The emotions seen in "living without the dead" are present in this stage, also. But they are somewhat different.

Sorrow is not so intense. When the widow feels that he/she is carrying on the life of the dead, there is less reason to mourn. In fact, the relaxation of sorrow is one of the hidden dynamics for persons who seek to live for the dead. Unconsciously they realize that they can escape the bitterness of sorrow by preserving their loved ones through their own lives.

Loneliness is present in just about the same way as described under "living without the dead." However, it tends to increase rather than to decrease over the months. This will be particularly true if the widow has neglected to build up new support systems because of his/her preoccupation with living for the dead. Eventually the widow must come to realize that these efforts are in vain. Then his/her loneliness is even greater. Now the widow is deprived of both the consolation of working for the dead and the support of friends.

Fear is present. There is the fear of living without the dead, and there is anxiety over not being able to carry out the desires of the dead. If the widow fails to carry out these projects perfectly, he/she generally feels a high degree of anxiety.

Anxiety can be defined as formless fear. That definition fits this situation very well. The widow's standards are self-imposed.

He/she demands perfection in carrying on the life of the dead. To fall short of these standards produces anxiety, which is often extreme. But there is no way to alleviate it. Since the widow's standards are self-imposed, there is no one else to blame for failure. So fear mounts, along with anger and guilt.

Anger may be felt toward persons who have not cooperated in the widow's effort to carry out the wishes of the dead. In most cases this anger is not warranted. Living persons should not be bound by the wishes, real or imagined, of dead persons. But the refusal of the living to be so bound is often interpreted by the widow as betrayal of the dead. This anger is often a source of the widow's alienation from friends and associates. That alienation feeds the widow's anger and loneliness.

Anger also will be self-directed in the form of *guilt.* Guilt is an important part of "living for the dead." As has been seen, the widow cannot really live for the dead. His/her failure in this effort arouses guilt feelings. Perhaps guilt played a part in setting up this stage. If so, the guilt will be acute when there is failure.

Guilt feelings, along with frustration,

may trigger *depression.* This is one of the most painful and least understood reactions in the grief process. It does not appear just in the stage of "living for the dead." It may come at the beginning of the process. Usually it then is the result of long, exhausted watching by the bedside of a terminally ill patient. Or it may be a reaction to an unexpected and untimely death.

Later in the process it may be triggered by a sense of frustration in seeking to live without the dead, and by loss of meaning and selfhood experienced in that stage. Or it may come toward the end of the grief process. Then it likely is the result of the widow's failure in efforts to live for the dead.

Depression is described as a period of emptiness and futility. Madden has described depression as a period when "what we give is worthless, what we do is useless, what we think is futile."[2]

Depression is characterized by an emotional tone of persistent gloom and pessimism. There is a loss of physical and emotional energy. It is difficult to get started at anything. The person has trouble thinking clearly and concentrating. There is loss of appetite and often severe insomnia, along with waking early in the morning. The person does not express any kind of emotion, even finding it difficult to cry.

This is a frightening state, especially for persons who have never experienced anything like it. But it probably is nature's way of dealing with overwhelming emotions or continual frustration. The person suffers loss of energy physically, mentally, and emotionally. Thus he/she is forced to quiet down and hibernate emotionally.

There is no cure for depression. Medication can be prescribed for the insomnia and the depressed feelings. But this only alleviates the symptoms. Over a period of time the person begins to recover strength physically. Then he/she can begin to cope with the emotions that have been shoved "on the back burner" during the depression. The person does not "snap out" of the depression. He/she gradually experiences a return of energy and life.

When the widow begins to come out of depression, he/she is generally in the same stage as when the depression occurred. But the mourner is now better able to deal with this stage. Life has moved along while the depression has seemed to slow down the mourner.

For instance, the depression may occur

at the loved one's death. It may last for some weeks. By that time many of the early experiences—the funeral, financial decisions, the probating of the will, and other adjustments—are past. The widow is just now beginning to mourn actively. But he/she is further down the line than if the mourning had begun immediately. Similar changes can be seen at whatever part of the grief process depression may occur.

When the person is moving back to a state of energy, he/she is better able to evaluate what has been going on. Persons who have been absorbed in "living for the dead" find during this period that they have been moving in a wrong direction. They have been forced by the depression to cease their efforts. Now they can see more clearly what they have been doing. This is the most healthy phase of "living for the dead." Through it the widow can make a new decision to cease these futile efforts. He/she can decide that it is all right to let go of the dead.

Signs of the End of the Mourning Phase

Whether the widow has been "living for the dead" or "living without the dead," or both, there comes a time when he/she truly accepts the death of the beloved in the emotional area of personality. There are certain signals that this acceptance is taking place:

1. A diminution of the emotions of sorrow, fear, anger, and loneliness;

2. The building of new support systems;

3. The ability to put the relationship with the dead person in the past; and

4. A redefinition of role that allows the person freedom to be himself/herself without reference to a marital partner.

When the widow has come to this point, he/she is usually at the stage of acceptance. There is a sense of peace over what has happened. There is a new ability to look toward the future without fear or regret. This kind of acceptance is the bridge between grief and new life.

Unfortunately, some persons never seem to reach this stage. For them acceptance is felt as *resignation*. They are resigned to the death but still feel it as a terrible void. For many such, the life ahead is not a full one. The wound is still present, even though almost healed. Such persons may linger in the latter stages of living without the dead or even try to continue some phase of living for the dead. They may need to have some external event, such as a new love interest or a change of job, to bring them out of resignation to new life.

For the one who has done grief work thoroughly and honestly, the prospect of new life is a joyous one. This person is ready for the last stage of grief work.

4
Grief Work—
Final Stage

Living Beyond Death

When acceptance comes as a sense of peace, the mourner is ready to move on to the final stage of grief work. He/she feels at peace with himself/herself and with the fact of death. There is still sadness over the loss, but it no longer occupies center stage in the person's life. Now there is hope for the future, because the person is ready to live in the present. He/she is willing to let the dead past bury its dead.

The Legacy of Grief Work

Grief has bound the person up with death. With the end of the grief process, the person is free to live again. Mourning makes it possible for the widow to surrender what has been invested in the dead person. With the acceptance of that loss, the widow's life can be reinvested.

And there is much to reinvest. The bereaved person who has worked creatively through the grief process has new resources available. He/she has developed new support systems. He/she has found new sources of internal strength.

The experience of grief is a deepening process. The person who has moved through grief to the other side knows much more than before. There is a new understanding of the healing which tears and sorrow bring. There is new sympathy for all those who mourn. There is the recognition that anger, guilt, and hostility can be faced honestly and overcome.

Fears need not be so frightening. One who has faced the ultimate fear of death can recognize the difference between the trivial and the significant. He/she is better able to find security in enduring values rather than in what is transient.

The widow may also recognize that, while he/she cannot live for the dead, much of the dead still is alive in the survivor. What has been shared has left a deposit in the living partner's personality. The best of what is deposited can be affirmed by the widow in his/her own life.

The loss of meaning that comes with widowhood can also be overcome by a recognition of what has been gained through the experiences of grief. The widowed person now has a chance to establish new personal goals. He/she may even be able to go back in time and resurrect dreams and plans that were put aside for the sake of marriage and family. This is an opportunity to make creative use of the time left to the surviving spouse.

Creative Possibilities in Widowhood

The widow has some advantages over the married person. We do not often think of these advantages, since the problems of widowhood have been so much emphasized. But there are advantages.

There are fewer taboos and expectations for the widowed person. Single persons can go to concerts, sporting events, eat out, and go on trips by themselves. For married persons to do so would mean the raising of eyebrows and questions about the health of the marriage. Many married persons deny themselves certain pleasures because these tastes are not shared by their mates. Or they endure certain events in order to please their mates. Widowed persons are freed from such expectations.

Widows are also free to choose their own life-styles. An early-morning person can get up at 5 AM without disturbing another. A late-night person can read or watch TV till 3 AM. Widows can decide when and what to eat, the kind of clothes to wear, and so on, without reference to a mate's prejudices. These ideas may sound selfish, but they can be used constructively. As persons fulfill their own desires, they can discover more of who they really are.

The widow has more time and more leisure (unless there are children in the home). He/she can decide how to use time profitably and pleasurably. There are many options open to persons who are willing to invest time in new ways. And there may be more money available, because there is only one person to use it.

A wise use of all these options can move the widow into new areas of living. In a sense, a recovery from grief is a rebirth. And a rebirth opens the way to a new life.

A number of creative possibilities are open to the widow who is willing to explore them. Not all these possibilities are feasible for each person. Age, health, and the circumstances in which the person lives may be limiting factors. But I am convinced that there are more possibilities for widows than many of them imagine. Here are some areas for considerations.

New relationships of love.—Probably the first thought that comes to mind here is the possibility of remarriage. In fact, this is the major hope that is held out to most widows. But if it is the only hope, the lack of a new partner can be terribly frustrating. Fortunately, there are many other possible relationships which are life-enriching.

The widow is now part of a new world—the one designated as "singles." But he/she also maintains ties to the world of the married. It may not be possible to hold on to all the old married friendships. But it is possible to have relationships with both married and single persons, if these are contracted on an individual basis. Perhaps widowed persons are in the best position to bring both worlds together. I have found much pleasure in giving dinner parties to which I invited both singles and marrieds. And I have invited some married individuals whose spouses could not attend for various reasons.

Also, the widow need not be bound by an age group. It is stimulating to make friends of different ages. For the older widow such relationships are insurance against losing friends. Too often I have heard older people lament that all their friends were "dying off." If some of their friends were always ten to fifteen years younger, this sort of attrition would not happen.

Widows may find their lives enhanced by becoming increasingly part of the "family of God." Our emphasis on the small, nuclear family has reduced our dependence on our extended earthly family. The mobility of American families has contributed to the decline in the importance of extended-family ties. In the church the widow can find a true extended family. He/she can find brothers, sisters, parents, nieces, nephews, and "cousins by the dozens" among church members.

Each Christmas my church provides for a "family of God" sharing experience. Families with children are joined by single persons and couples in groups of about eight to ten. These groups make up fruit baskets for shut-in members of the church. Each group takes about three or four shut-ins. They carry the baskets to the shut-in members, sing carols, and wish them a Merry Christmas. This sharing across family and generational lines, both among the carolers and the older shut-in members, gives an extra "family" touch to our Christmas celebrations. Friends of both sexes and all ages may be found by joining special-interest groups. These may be hobby clubs, political groups, and social service organizations. Persons who share the same interests have a basis for companionship. Many abiding friendships are made in this way.

There are many options for friendships. And the widow has much to share: of life, of joy and sorrow, of love.

New meaning in life.—Renewal of life offers opportunity for finding new meaning in life. Former obligations and responsibilities may be gone. This void can be filled by life-enriching activities.

The widow may find a new job or new ways to enhance his/her present job. There may be opportunity to develop an avocation which the person has long found appealing but had no time to work with. Often persons turn such avocations into "second careers."

There is always opportunity for more education. A person may complete a degree, take graduate study, or engage in the numerous adult education programs available in many communities.

Service to others is a live option. Most women spend most of their lives caring for others. When they are widowed, this outlet may seem closed. But there are many needs for service in every community. Men, too, may find much joy in service. Most men have not had time for such activities. With more time on their hands, they can engage in community service. Many men have business and committee-work skills that are invaluable to social service and community betterment groups.

Travel is another way of adding meaning to life. More travel plans are being developed which make provision for the single traveler. Many people have never seen much of the beauties of our own country. In spite of the dollar's performance abroad, trips overseas are still possible. Many travel packages give good rates.

Taking advantage of new opportunities requires courage. But the widow has already conquered fears more devastating than these. When one has learned to cope with death and with living again, one can have self-confidence and faith in stepping into the unknown.

New self-identity.—This is perhaps the most basic and often the least grasped option for the widow.

Most of us, if not all, take our identities from our roles in life. A man typically takes his identity from his work role. When asked, "Who are you?" he will generally answer: "I'm . . . . I work at . . . ."

A woman typically takes her identity from her husband, especially if she does not have an identity outside the home. When asked, "Who are you?" she will usually answer, "I'm Mrs. . . ." She does not use her given name, but her husband's. If pressed further for her identity, she will either describe herself as a mother or tell something about her husband's job, it if is one that confers status.

Widowhood destroys the role of wife or husband. If persons have invested much of their identities in these roles, they may feel as if they have also lost their selfhood with the loss of a mate. This is a frightening situation. But it is also a time when persons can discover their own unique identities.

Most people do not stop to think of their inherent worth as persons. We are all so used to establishing identity through roles or through comparison with others that we do not look at ourselves as unique individuals.

Human uniqueness is validated in two ways. One way is theological: Human beings are made in the image of God. And God does not make duplicates. If every leaf on a tree shows individual differences, how much more will each person, made in God's image, be special and unique!

The other way of validating uniqueness is biological: Geneticists tell us that the particular combination of genes that produces a human individual has never been and will never be duplicated. Even identical twins with the same set of genes are different in personality. They have their own unique set of fingerprints, their special ways of reacting to the world, and their special gifts.

These truths are mind-staggering. The person who really accepts them can never look at himself/herself again as someone of little worth.

Since each person is unique, each has much to contribute to the world. And each one has many possibilities for growth and development as a person.

During the grief process and afterward, the widow has been forced into more introspection and self-knowledge than he/she has probably engaged in for many years. The widow can look at the potentials, both

of strength and weakness, that have been
discovered. He/she can recognize the
uniqueness of personality. This opens the
way to make a new assessment of identity.
And this identity can be one based on individual worth, not on roles or status. As the
person does so, new avenues of growth in
personhood can be discovered. Often widows unconsciously do this, and they blos-
som as individuals. What they have done is
to affirm themselves as persons.

Those who come to this self-knowledge
are also in a good position to form new relationships and to find new meaning in life.
They are also the ones best equipped to en-
ter into a new marriage.

Every person who loses a mate is
changed by the experience. Those who seek
to recreate the former relationship by finding a mate who will reinforce the old life-
style often set themselves up for disappoint-
ment. The healthy remarriage is the one
based on present reality. It is the one where
a person, knowing himself/herself in a new
way, seeks a mate who will fit that personality. For such persons a new marriage is a
creative experience.

All these creative possibilities carry with
them the emotions of love and joy. There

may be love to others. There may be love expended in meaningful activities. There will certainly be an increased love for oneself.

And overflowing joy is possible to the widow who lives beyond death. The person who enjoys life to the full, having lived with death, is the one who knows what life is all about. Such persons can say with the psalmist:

> Weeping may tarry for the night,
> but joy comes with the morning (Ps. 30:5, RSV).

The night of sorrow is for weeping. The song of joy is for the dawn of a day. This day is meant to be lived to the full, because it is given by God.

Notes

Introduction

1. Myron Madden, *Raise the Dead!* (Waco, Texas: Word, Inc., 1975), 34.
2. Virginia Barckley, RN, "Grief, a Part of Living," *Ohio's Health,* 20:34-38, 1968.

Chapter Two

1. Madden, 36-39.
2. Elisabeth Kubler-Ross, *On Death and Dying* (New York: The Macmillan Company, 1969), 168.

Chapter Three

1. Madden, 34-36.
2. Madden, 42.

Bibliography

Brown, H. C. Jr., *A Search for Strength* (Waco, Texas: Word Books, 1967). Out of print. One man's story of his search for resources to cope with the loss of a wife.

__________, *Walking Toward Your Fear* (Nashville: Broadman Press, 1972). The story of one man's triumph over his personal fears—of invalidism, death, and bereavement.

Claypool, John R., *Tracks of a Fellow Struggler* (Waco: Word, Inc., 1974). Sermons preached by a pastor struggling with the terminal illness and death of a beloved child.

Jackson, Edgar N., *Understanding Grief* (Nashville: Abingdon Press, 1957). A classic on the emotions and reactions of grief.

Kubler-Ross, Elisabeth, *On Death and Dying* (New York: The Macmillan Company; copyright 1969 by Elisabeth Kubler-Ross). The definitive book on the reactions of dying patients and their families to the imminence of death.

Kutscher, Austin, ed., *But Not to Lose* (copyright 1969, by Austin Kutscher). Various persons discuss the aspects of bereavement, from the funeral to the final resolution of grief.

Madden, Myron C., *Raise the Dead!* (Waco, Texas: Word, Inc., 1975). The author discusses grief as the process of letting go of the dead and finding newness of life.

Oates, Wayne E., *Anxiety in Christian Experience* (Philadelphia: Westminster Press, 1955). A study of the meaning and experience of anxiety. Chapters 2-3 deal with anxiety as it is related to death and grief.

Parkes, Colin Murray, *Bereavement: Studies of Grief in Adult Life* (New York: Tavistock Institute of Human Relations, 1972). A study of widowed persons (women) and their reaction to bereavement.

Stoddard Sandol, *The Hospice Movement: A Better Way of Caring for the Dying* (New York: Vintage Books; copyright 1978 by Sandol Stoddard). Discusses the hospice as a way of helping dying persons (usually the terminally ill) find comfort and assurance in their last months.

Switzer, David K., *The Dynamics of Grief* (Nashville: Abingdon Press, 1970). A careful study of the emotions of grief, drawing on many other definitive studies in this field.

Westburg, Granger, *Good Grief* (Philadelphia: Fortress Press, 1971). A very brief, but helpful, book on the emotions and the process of grief. Excellent for giving to persons who mourn.

There are many other fine books by Christian widows—men and women—detailing their individual journeys through grief.